# Fruits of the Holy Spirit

Copyright ©2021
Contact address: Oteng Montshiti
P O Box M1139
Kanye
Botswana

E-mail address: otengmontshiti@gmail.com
Contact number: (+267) 74 644 954

# **Contents**

Introduction... 4

## *Chapter 1*
Love... 7

## *Chapter 2*
Joy... 10

## *Chapter 3*
Patience...12

## *Chapter 4*
Peace... 14

## *Chapter 5*
Self- control...17

## *Chapter 6*
Goodness... 20

## **Chapter 7**
Kindness... 23

## *Chapter 8*
Faithfulness...25

## *Chapter 9*
Meekness or humility... 27

## <u>Acknowledgements</u>

Writing a book is a challenging task which requires time. I would like thank my family especially my lovely wife for supporting me.

# Fruits of the Holy Spirit

**Galathians 5:22** But the fruit of the Spirit is love, joy, peace, patience, kindness, goodness, faithfulness,

# Introduction

**John 15:1** I am the true vine, and my Father is the husbandman.

**John 15:2** Every branch in me that beareth not fruit he taketh away: and every *branch* that beareth fruit, he purgeth it, that it may bring forth more fruit.

**John 15:3** Now ye are clean through the word which I have spoken unto you.

**John 15:4** Abide in me, and I in you. As the branch cannot bear fruit of itself, except it abide in the vine; no more can ye, except ye abide in me.

**John 15:5** I am the vine, ye *are* the branches: He that abideth in me, and I in him, the same bringeth forth much fruit: for without me ye can do nothing.

**John 15:6** If a man abide not in me, he is cast forth as a branch, and is withered; and men gather them, and cast *them* into the fire, and they are burned.

**John 15:7** If ye abide in me, and my words abide in you, ye shall ask what ye will, and it shall be done unto you.

**John 15:8** Herein is my Father glorified, that ye bear much fruit; so shall ye be my disciples.

The fruits of the spirit manifest in our lives as we cultivate our relationship with Jesus Christ. They come from having a relationship or fellowship with the Holy Spirit or Jesus Christ because the Bible says; He is the vine and we are the branches. When we remain connected to him, we will bear fruits, and that's what the fruits of the Holy Spirit are.

When you are guided by the spirit of God, you bear them. For example, when you are walking in a mall and you meet abandoned or street children, the spirit of God will tell you to give them something. If you obey His voice and help them, you are showing and manifesting the spirit of compassion and kindness, which are the fruits of the spirit of the living God.

# **Chapter 1**
## Love

**1John 4:7** Beloved, let us love one another: for love is of God; and every one that loveth is born of God, and knoweth God.

**1John 4:8** He that loveth not knoweth not God; for God is love.

Love is the nature of God and it is the greatest and the umbrella word that distinguishes Him from our enemy, the devil. To look at somebody who isn't successful and have a heart of giving it takes the spirit of love to do so. To help other students in your class that are struggling, it takes love to help them get out of their predicament. And God almighty expects each one of us to operate by love. It takes love to pray for your worst enemies, and it takes godly love to do so. People who don't have love in their hearts always want to even the scores when other people have wounded them.

That isn't how children of God are expected to operate or behave. When people have wronged you, try by all means to engage in diplomatic dialogue and it takes the spirit of love to do so.

If you want the world to be a better place for you and children not yet born, allow the spirit of love to live in your heart. You won't impose your faith on other people. You will allow them to digest what you have shared with them and make an educated decision. People are backsliding from different faiths because they were forced to accept them.

Love is the only tool that can make you respect other people's choices in life. Love is the nature of God. That's the main reason He gave up Jesus Christ to die for our sins at the cross of Calvary because of His unconditional love towards humanity. He does everything under the sun and heaven out of love Without it, he can't function. To bless you with whatever you have been asking from him, he is doing that out of it.

If you want God to use you mightily, you must operate by love. Because He won't entrusts anybody with the power to heal, deliver, restore if he or she lacks godly love because His power is needed more by people who are non-believers to show them He cares about them and is on the throne.

# Chapter 2
## Joy

**John 15:11** These things have I spoken unto you, that my joy might remain in you, and *that* your joy might be full.

**Romans 5:11** And not only *so*, but we also joy in God through our Lord Jesus Christ, by whom we have now received the atonement.

It is the heartbeat of God for his children to be filled with joy that's one of the fruits of the spirit of God living or dwelling in your heart you will experience joy on the inside. To have the spirit of joy circulating in your heart doesn't eliminates situations or challenges to surface across your path but you must know that what you are passing through is temporary and be filled with the spirit of joy in your heart. God says in his word that you shouldn't be troubled or worried because it's His sincere heart desire to answer your prayers and experience joy in your life. However, one e thing is certain: before God you have been given the power of choice, you can choose to live a joyful life or walk down the path of sorrow or pain. As a covenant child of God who dwells in the dimension of eternity, He wants you to be filled with joy as you stroll along the road of challenges.

Never allow the devil to deceive you and fill your heart with tainted thoughts. Remember, God is on the throne. He loves you and embrace His love, and the spirit of joy will set in. When you allow the Holy Spirit to guide you, it will just manifest in your life. It is as easy as that. Nothing to struggle about.

# <u>Chapter 3</u>
## <u>Patience</u>

**James 1:4** But let patience have *her* perfect
work, that ye may be perfect and entire,
wanting nothing.

Under the sun or heaven, it's the heart's
desire of every man to achieve his dreams.
But sometimes we want things to happen
according to our schedule or calendar, which
is wrong. Sometimes answers seem to delay
but be of good cheer. The answer to your
situation is on the way. Don't give up on God
or your dreams.

When you want to establish something in
your life, you must exercise patience, which is
one of the fruits of the spirit of God. Under
heaven, you are going to face difficulties. If
you are a student and you have failed in the
past, be patient, your breakthrough is
coming. Keep on working hard. Every child of
God is expected to be patient in whatever he
or she does.

In life, the master key to overcoming challenges is the spirit of patience. If you want to start your business, be patient because God operates according to his will, times, and seasons. If you put your time aside and allow God almighty to guide you, the sky is the limit.

For example, Jesus Christ started his ministry at thirty. Moses had to spend forty years in the house of Jethro. It wasn't easy, but one thing sustained them and it's the spirit of patience. They knew that their time didn't count before God. Only his time was the best. As we are racing towards the end of things, don't give up have patience with God and your reward awaits you in heaven. Many people have given up on God and seek help from alternative sources and when you ask them why? The answer is quite simple, lack of patience, and it has destroyed many lives. However, we thank God almighty for the Holy Spirit who comforts, guides us as we do that the fruit of patience manifests in our lives as His children.

# Chapter 4
## Peace

**Psalm 4:8** I will both lay me down in peace, and sleep: for thou, LORD, only makest me dwell in safety.

**Isaiah 26:3** Thou wilt keep *him* in perfect peace, *whose* mind *is* stayed *on thee*: because he trusteth in thee.

**John 14:27** Peace I leave with you, my peace I give unto you: not as the world giveth, give I unto you. Let not your heart be troubled, neither let it be afraid.

When you have the Holy Spirit in your heart, one thing that is going to manifest in your life is peace. The peace that the word of God is talking about doesn't mean you are going to be immune from challenges or situations. But it is going to sustain you as you racing through situations of life. The world can't give that peace. It is only found in Jesus Christ, the princes of peace.

When you aren't born again, you can't experience the peace that flows down from the throne of God to your heart. It is beyond human understanding. There is a bird that loves storms, which is known as an eagle. When rain clouds gather, twist, and somersault on the horizon, it jumps into the storm without fear and celebrates because it knows that promotion is coming. That's the inner peace that the word of God is talking about. When you are passing through a rough patch in your life, inner peace is the only tool that is going to sustain you. That's why Jesus Christ told his disciples that "I give you peace not as the world does."

When you have inner peace, you are operating from the position of dominion. People who lack it are always troubled in their hearts and never enjoy dominion over their circumstances. Instead, they dominate them. That's why when a racing storm erupted in the sea, Jesus Christ stood on the boat, rebuked the wind and there was calmness. Do you know why? It's because he had inner peace in his heart and when you have it, you are automatically a winner.

So, if you want to experience inner peace, just keep on believing the word of God and everything will be alright.

# Chapter 5
## Self-control

**1Corithians 9:25** And every man that striveth for the mastery is temperate in all things. Now they *do it* to obtain a corruptible crown; but we an incorruptible.

As a covenant child of God, the Holy Spirit is going to give you the grace to exercise self-control. You are expected to tame your flesh. That's to say, you must take dominion over the desire of the flesh, like sexual immorality, and so on. You shouldn't yield to them. One thing should be made clear, your flesh is under your control as a child of the living God.

Self-control doesn't end there. It includes controlling your emotions like anger and responding to situations calmly and wisely. People who lack self-control, get angry, frustrated and so on easily. However, as a child of God, you have the living God and you can take control of your emotions by his grace. For example, when Jesus Christ was arrested, he didn't fly into a rage. To make matters interesting, he even rebuked Peter for not controlling his emotions when he cut another person's ear. He was disappointed because a few minutes later; he had instructed them to be in the spirit of prayer to avoid temptations. If you are connected to the spirit of God, you will always have self-control, no matter what life throws at you.

Lack of self-control can destroy your destiny. To achieve your godly destiny or purpose, you need the spirit of the Lord to guide you and to have self-control. If you aren't careful, you may cripple your bright future. For example, lack of self-control or short temper cost Prophet Moses the grace to lead the children of Israel into Canaan, the Land of milk and honey. His weakness was recorded to learn from his life.

In life, you shouldn't respond to every attack that is coming your way. Just relax and respond when necessary. Sometimes you have to let things happen and surrender them to God. That's the greatest weapon at your disposal as the child of God. And it takes the spirit of self-control to do so.

# __Chapter 6__
## __Goodness__

**Galatians 6:10** As we have therefore opportunity, let us do good unto all *men*, especially unto them who are of the household of faith.

**Luke 6:30** Give to every man that asketh of thee; and of him that taketh away thy goods ask *them* not again.

**Psalm 23:6** Surely goodness and mercy shall follow me all the days of my life: and I will dwell in the house of the LORD forever.

As a child of God, you should know that His goodness surrounds you wherever you go. That's to say, his kindness, mercy, and forgiveness are what you should portray as you are walking with other people. Remember, his goodness and mercy endures forever. The word goodness comes from the word good. To be good means to treat other people with compassion and from the goodness of your heart.

A good heart is ready to forgive and forget and celebrate when other people are climbing the ladder of success. It's a heart that wishes others well. Not whereby you complain and become jealous when your fellow brethren testify about the goodness of God concerning their lives.

A good heart attracts God. He will never tolerate or dwell in a heart that has been tainted with bitterness, jealousy, self-doubt, and so on. These are the tools that the Devil uses to weigh you down. So it's of paramount importance to wash them away or get rid of them from your heart, to be in a state of goodness, which is one fruit of the spirit of God.

As a child of God, you must treat others with the goodness and kindness they deserve. God has also instructed us to treat other people with goodness. You can't produce it on your own because there are two types of goodness, namely divine and natural goodness. Natural goodness is done with personal efforts or without the Holy Spirit involved. While divine one is done under the influence of the Spirit of God.

# Chapter 7
## Kindness

**Colossians 3:12** Put on therefore, as the elect of God, holy and beloved, bowels of mercies, kindness, humbleness of mind, meekness, longsuffering;

What motivated Jesus Christ to perform miracles, signs, and wonders was the spirit of kindness or compassion. That's why he fed five thousand people with two bread and five fishes. That's why he raised the dead, heal the sick and mend the broken-hearted.

As a child of God, you are supposed to be an imitator of Jesus Christ or the word of God. You mustn't look away when you see the needy, orphans, widows, widowers, and streets children. You must be moved by compassion and kindness to smile at them and help them get out of their predicaments. As a child of God, try by all means to give them a sense of hope in life.

When you meet a sick person, don't look away, ask his or her permission and pray for him or her. If situations permit, you can lay your hands upon him or her, and healing will take place by the special grace of God.

When you are checking somebody at a hospital, ask others within his or her ward and pray with them. That's how compassion or kindness operates. Somebody who has the spirit of kindness never looks away when he or she meets a situation he or she can address or solve. If you are working in a government department, a client hasn't been helped within the stipulated time, make sure you help her or him in any way you can. That's compassion and kindness.

# Chapter 8
## Faithfulness

**Matthews 21:22** And all things, whatsoever ye shall ask in prayer, believing, ye shall receive.

As you are walking with the Lord and his spirit guides you, the spirit of faithfulness is going to manifest in your life. You are going to realize that God wants you to be faithful to Him and other people all the time. And also that He is faithful all the time to his word and he will fulfil all his promises concerning your life.

I always tell people that nobody can be faithful to others without being faithful to God first. You can't be faithful to your wife if you can't be faithful to the word of God. Because everything good starts with God and flows to others.

As God's child, you must be faithful to other people. You must fulfil whatever you have promised them. Faithfulness is one of the fruits of the spirit this generation doesn't want, but if you have it on the inside, you will keep or fulfil your promises. And you won't promise people what you don't have.

As a child of the living God, you shouldn't promise God what you won't fulfil. For example, you shouldn't promise Him that you will take care of the orphans, widows, widowers, and street children when He blesses you and fails to keep your word. If you promise Him in your heart that you will sweep His house or church every Sunday or Saturday, the spirit of faithfulness is going to tell you to keep your words. If you have promised Him to donate something to his church, it will tell you to fulfil your promise because God doesn't tolerate liars. The spirit of faithfulness tells you to keep your word so that other people can trust you.

# Chapter 9
## Meekness or humility

**1Peter 3:4** But *let it be* the hidden man of the heart, in that which is not corruptible, *even the ornament* of a meek and quiet spirit, which is in the sight of God of great price.

**1Peter 5:5** Likewise, ye younger, submit yourselves unto the elder. Yea, all *of you* be subject one to another, and be clothed with humility: for **God resisteth the proud, and giveth grace to the humble.**

**Matthews 5:5** Blessed *are* the meek: for they shall inherit the earth.

Somebody who is humble or meek has a teachable spirit. That's to say, it is somebody who allows himself or herself to be taught, corrected, or rebuked without flying into a rage. It is somebody who allows the word of God to guide or influence his or her conduct or character. When such people are on the verge of evening the scores with their enemies, they allow the spirit of forgiveness and reconciliation to rule them.

People who have the spirit of meekness review their conduct regularly. That's to say, they play the events of the day over and over in their heads while lying in their beds at night and ask forgiveness from God for what they have done wrong during the day. They don't justify their actions before Him when they have wronged other people. They apologize, and it takes the spirit of humility or meekness to do that.

For example, when you have wronged your brethren in the house of God, the leadership might call both of you, and it takes humility to listen to them and apologize. When you are asked to clean the church, working place, and so on, it takes humility to carry out your task without complaining and murmuring.

Further, it takes humility to work under you boss who is less educated than you, listen to his instructions, and obey them to the lette without complaining or disrespecting him o her.

However, if you lack it, you are going to question his or her integrity as a leader. You are going to undermine their authority. If you lack it, you won't amount to anything because you are going to kill your destiny prematurely.

Humility means putting other people's needs before yours.

# The end

Lightning Source UK Ltd.
Milton Keynes UK
UKRC010659220921
390774UK00010B/75